ABUNDANT TRUTH INTERNATIONAL MINISTRIES

Kingdom Discipleship Series

Power for Kingdom Service

Exploring the Gifts and Ministries of the Kingdom

Roderick Levi Evans

Published by Abundant Truth Publishing
P.O. Box 126 * Camden, NC 27921
Phone: 1-877-841-7209 * Fax: 1-877-841-7209
Web: www.abundantpublishing.net
Email: abundantpublishing@gmail.com

Printed U.S.A.

Front & Back Cover Designs by Abundant Truth Publishing

> Abundant Truth Publishing is a ministry of Abundant Truth International Ministries. The primary mission of ATI Ministries is to equip the Body of Christ with tools necessary to defend and contend for the truth of the Christian faith. Jesus Christ came to bear witness of the truth and ATI Ministries is a modern-day extension of His commission (John 18:37).

Power for Kingdom Service: Exploring the Gifts and Ministries of the Kingdom
©2024 Abundant Truth Publishing
All Rights Reserved

ISBN13: 978-1-60141-544-8

Unless otherwise indicated, all of the scripture quotations are taken from the *Authorized King James Version* of the Bible. Scripture quotations marked with NIV are taken from the *New International Version* of the Bible. Scripture quotations marked with NASV are taken from the *New American Standard Version* of the Bible. Scripture quotations marked with Amplified are taken from the *Amplified Bible*.

Contents

Introduction

Chapter 1 - Apostle   1

Apostles are Sent Ones   3

Apostolic Ministry Diversities   5

Chapter 2 – Prophet   13

Prophets and the Scriptures   15

Prophets and the Divine Intention   17

Chapter 3 - Evangelist   25

The Preaching of the Evangelist   28

Contents (cont.)

The Power of the Evangelist — 30

Chapter 4 – Pastor — 35

The Work of Pastors — 38

The Warning to Pastors — 40

Chapter 5 – Teacher — 45

The Mandate of the Teacher — 47

The Miraculous and the Teacher — 50

Chapter 6 - The Gifts of the Spirit — 55

Gifts of Revelation — 57

Contents *(cont.)*

Gifts of Inspiration 61

Gifts of Power 66

Bibliography 71

Scripture References 73

Introduction

Jesus called His followers disciples. A **disciple** is a convinced adherent of a school or individual who accepts and assists in spreading the doctrines of another. A Christian must not only believe on Jesus but be willing to share the faith of Jesus Christ. In order to do this, the believer has to not only understand his role as a disciple but know how to defend his beliefs.

The Kingdom Discipleship Series explores the biblical truths that should assist the believer in developing as a disciple of Christ. Not only will Christians grow in their walk with the Lord, but their understanding of foundational biblical truths will also expand.

In this issue

Every kingdom has officials and leaders. The Kingdom of God has officials also. God has set these officials in the Church. Unlike their counterparts in the world, officials in the Kingdom must serve those in the Kingdom.

Oftentimes, there is no honor given to those who hold positions of the Kingdom of God. However, we must thank God for them. God has placed men and women in the Kingdom of God that we can learn from and follow. They are our gifts. He takes the lives of men and women and turns them upside down so that they can minister to us. God has placed them in the Body of Christ to help edify and strengthen us in our walk with God.

> *As every man hath received the gift, even so minister the same one toward another, as good stewards of the manifold grace of God. If any man speak, let him speak as the oracles of God. If any man ministers, let him do it as of*

the ability which God giveth; that God in all things may be glorified through Jesus Christ, to whom be praise and dominion forever and ever. Amen. (I Peter 4:10-11)

Each of these ministries carries with it certain gifts, functions, and responsibilities. We look at briefly at each of these ministries to understand God's purpose for them in the Body.

POWER FOR KINGDOM SERVICE

-Chapter 1-

Apostle

POWER FOR KINGDOM SERVICE

POWER FOR KINGDOM SERVICE

Apostles are foundation layers in the Kingdom of God. They help to prepare the way for upcoming moves of God. The authority they possess in the Spirit characterizes their ministry. They have revelation and insight for the Church.

Apostles are Sent Ones

Paul referred to the apostles as ambassadors. They are sent to represent the King of Kings. Let us consider some other key points about the apostolic office.

POWER FOR KINGDOM SERVICE

They help to establish churches in the faith of Christ. Apostles exercise oversight in the Kingdom of God. Paul and his companions traveled extensively strengthening and establishing churches. They exercised authority over churches they established and even over churches that were established by others.

And so were the churches established in the faith and increased in number daily. (Acts 16:5)

POWER FOR KINGDOM SERVICE

Apostolic Ministry Diversities

Not all Apostles have the same ministry. We learn from the scriptures that the apostles had different formats in which they operated in their ministries. We see apostles (like Paul and Barnabas) who traveled, established churches, and preached more than any others to the Gentiles.

On the other hand, we see apostles like James, the Lord's brother, who seemed to be more stationary having oversight over the church at

POWER FOR KINGDOM SERVICE

Jerusalem.

But contrariwise, when they saw that the gospel of the uncircumcision was committed unto me, as the gospel of the circumcision was unto Peter; (For he that wrought effectually in Peter to the apostleship of the circumcision, the same was mighty in me toward the Gentiles). (Galatians 2:7-8)

They exercise great authority in the Spirit realm. God has invested His very own authority into the ministry of the apostle. They act as overseers

POWER FOR KINGDOM SERVICE

in the Spirit. As overseers, they can execute the judgment and discipline of God.

Of whom is Hymeneus and Alexander; whom I have delivered unto Satan, that they may learn not to blaspheme. (I Timothy 1:20)

They have signs and wonders following their ministry. The Lord always confirmed the ministry of the apostles with signs and wonders. Signs and wonders accompanied their ministry as a testimony of the

POWER FOR KINGDOM SERVICE

resurrection.

Signs and wonders will always point us to Christ. Apostolic ministry should always show the Lordship of Christ.

> *And by the hands of the apostles were any signs and wonders wrought among the people; and they were all with one accord in Solomon's porch. (Acts 5:12)*

However, apostles must be careful not to abuse their authority. Apostles have to be aware not to operate out of

POWER FOR KINGDOM SERVICE

a harsh and controlling spirit. The authority that God has given them must be tempered with love and compassion.

POWER FOR KINGDOM SERVICE

POWER FOR KINGDOM SERVICE

Notes:

POWER FOR KINGDOM SERVICE

_____

_____

_____

_____

_____

_____

_____

_____

_____

_____

POWER FOR KINGDOM SERVICE

-Chapter 2-

Prophet

POWER FOR KINGDOM SERVICE

Prophets and Prophetesses are the spokespeople for God. They bring the heart and mind of God to the Church. They will operate in a greater prophetic realm than those who have the gift of prophecy. They will be men and women of the written word of God.

Prophets and the Scriptures

They must and will know the scriptures. They are powerful intercessors. Their ministries will also vary. The revelation of God and gifts of the Spirit will operate in them consistently and accurately. Let us examine a few other points about the prophetic office.

Their authority lies in the fact that they speak for God. Prophets have authority, but unlike the apostle, their authority is based solely on the fact that they are relaying God's words. It is for this reason that no prophet should speak except it is from the Lord.

And go, get thee to them of the captivity, unto the children of thy people, and speak unto them, and tell them, Thus saith the Lord God; whether they will hear, or whether they will forbear. But when I speak with thee, I will open thy mouth, and thou shalt say unto them, Thus saith the Lord God; He that heareth, let him hear; and he that forbeareth, let him forebear: for they are a rebellious house. (Ezekiel 3:11, 27)

Prophets and the Divine Intention

They have the ability to pronounce; that is, announce God's

POWER FOR KINGDOM SERVICE

judgment and blessing. They will not do this themselves. They will relay God's favor or displeasure.

True prophets of God will pronounce God's judgment. It has to be God's judgment and not their opinion. They will not be able to fulfill their duty without doing so.

See, I have this day set thee over the nations and over the kingdoms, to root out, and to pull down, and to destroy, and to throw down, to build, and to plant. (Jeremiah 1: 10)

Hearing the voice of the Lord through them brings prosperity. If you receive a word from a true prophet, you will advance in your walk with God. Prophets represent the heart of God. Receiving a God-sent word will only strengthen and encourage you, even if the word is to repent.

Jehoshaphat stood and said, Hear me, O Judah, and ye inhabitants of Jerusalem; Believe in the Lord God, so shall ye be established;

POWER FOR KINGDOM SERVICE

believe His prophets, so shall ye prosper. (2 Chronicles 20:20b)

Prophets must guard themselves against pride and divination. Many prophets fail in their ministries because they think more highly of themselves than they ought. They begin to take on a psychic spirit.

One sign of this is that they will not always have a "word" about everything. This means that a prophet will be restrained and disciplined. Though God speaks to and through

POWER FOR KINGDOM SERVICE

them regularly, they must only speak when He speaks.

POWER FOR KINGDOM SERVICE

POWER FOR KINGDOM SERVICE

Notes:

POWER FOR KINGDOM SERVICE

POWER FOR KINGDOM SERVICE

-Chapter 3-

Evangelist

POWER FOR KINGDOM SERVICE

POWER FOR KINGDOM SERVICE

The ministry of the evangelist is widely accepted. The evangelist's role is unique from all of the other ministries. This is because evangelists have a dual function. Their primary task is to proclaim the good news or gospel of Jesus Christ.

The duality lies in the fact that they are called to minister to both sinner and saint. The office of evangelist is listed as a ministry to help perfect the saints just as the other ministries. Other points about the

POWER FOR KINGDOM SERVICE

Evangelist.

The Preaching of the Evangelist

Evangelists are anointed and sent by God to preach the Gospel. Their primary ministry is to preach the good news of Jesus Christ.

How then shall they call on him in whom they have not believed? And how shall they believe in him of whom they have not heard? And how shall they hear without a preacher? And how shall they preach except they be sent? As it is written, How beautiful are the feet of them that preach the gospel of peace, and bring good tidings! (Romans 10:14-15)

They will be able, more so than any other ministry, to defend the gospel and compel individuals to give their lives to Christ.

The Spirit of the Lord is upon me, because he hath anointed me to preach the gospel to the poor; he hath sent me to heal the broken hearted, to preach deliverance to

POWER FOR KINGDOM SERVICE

the captives, and recovering of sight to the blind, to set at liberty them that are bruised, to preach the acceptable year of the Lord.(Luke 4:18-19)

The Power of the Evangelist

Healing, deliverance, and miracles should accompany their ministry. When Philip the evangelist preached in Samaria, deliverances and healings were manifest in his ministry. He serves as a pattern to evangelists today.

If you feel God has called you

POWER FOR KINGDOM SERVICE

to this ministry, pray for power or you will not be able to fully discharge your ministry.

And the people with one accord gave heed unto those things which Philip spake, hearing and seeing the miracles which he did. For unclean spirits, crying with a loud voice, came out of many that were possessed with them: and many taken with palsies, and that were lame, were healed. (Acts 8:6-7; 21:8)

POWER FOR KINGDOM SERVICE

Evangelists must be careful not to become lone rangers. Since most evangelists travel extensively, they can become their own leaders. They must strive to form healthy relationships in the Body of Christ, especially in local assemblies where they can be accountable.

This will protect them from themselves and every device of the adversary. In doing so, they will have fruitful ministries and bring great blessings to the Body of Christ.

POWER FOR KINGDOM SERVICE

Notes:

POWER FOR KINGDOM SERVICE

POWER FOR KINGDOM SERVICE

-Chapter 4-

Pastor

POWER FOR KINGDOM SERVICE

POWER FOR KINGDOM SERVICE

Pastors are the shepherds and overseers of the people of God. Their title describes their function; they care for the people of God in the Spirit, as a shepherd does sheep. They watch out for the souls of those whom they lead.

Pastors wear more hats than any of the other offices. They have to serve as counselors, preachers, teachers, intercessors, mediators, and the like. Consider some other points about the pastoral office:

POWER FOR KINGDOM SERVICE

The Work of Pastors

Pastors cause the people of God to grow/prosper through their ministry. They do this through their ministry of the Word. Their congregants should be able to feed and mature.

And I will set up shepherds over them which shall feed them: and they shall fear no more, nor be dismayed, neither shall they be lacking, saith the Lord. (Jeremiah 23:4)

Pastors lead by instruction and

POWER FOR KINGDOM SERVICE

example. We must follow. Along with the ministry of the Word, pastors must be examples. A natural shepherd does more leading than talking.

Even if the pastor has not said one word, the people of God should see the Word demonstrated in his lifestyle.

Remember them, which have the rule over you, who have spoken the word of God: whose faith follow, considering the end of the conversation. (Hebrews 13:7)

POWER FOR KINGDOM SERVICE

Pastors are to represent the heart of God and care for the Church. Pastors should take on the nature of the Good Shepherd. They are protectors over the flock of God and watchmen.

And I will give you pastors after mine own heart, which shall feed you with knowledge and understanding. (Jeremiah 3:15)

The Warning to Pastors

Pastors must guard against the Pharisaic spirit: preaching and teaching only for the praise of men.

POWER FOR KINGDOM SERVICE

They have to remember they are privileged to lead.

They must not look upon the people of God as their servants, but rather be ready to serve. In doing so, they and the people of God will grow into the fullness of the stature of Christ.

POWER FOR KINGDOM SERVICE

POWER FOR KINGDOM SERVICE

Notes:

POWER FOR KINGDOM SERVICE

POWER FOR KINGDOM SERVICE

-Chapter 5-

Teacher

POWER FOR KINGDOM SERVICE

POWER FOR KINGDOM SERVICE

Teachers are anointed to expound upon the word of God. Often times they are anointed apologists of the Word.

The Mandate of the Teacher

They will look at the Word: line upon line and precept upon precept. They possess the revelation knowledge of God concerning the scriptures.

Their ministry is devalued at times, but their ministry is very important. Let us look at their ministry more closely.

POWER FOR KINGDOM SERVICE

Teachers help the Church to grow through their ministry. Teachers provide systematic guidelines for living in the Kingdom. Apollos was a recognized teacher in the early church. The Corinthian church respected him as a teacher.

I have planted, Apollos watered; but God gave the increase. (I Corinthians 3:6) see also Acts 18:24 -28.

The office of the teacher is a vital ministry in the Church. Some

POWER FOR KINGDOM SERVICE

commentators have determined that Ephesians 4:11 should be read pastor-teacher instead of pastors and teachers. Therefore, it is not one of the significant ministry offices.

However, after God set apostles and prophets in the Church, He then placed teachers. This is so the Church can be grounded in Him.

We should not receive this ministry as boring or useless, it is vital to the foundation of the Church.

POWER FOR KINGDOM SERVICE

And God hath set some in the Church, apostles, secondarily prophets, thirdly teachers... (I Corinthians 12:28a)

Now there were in the Church at Antioch certain prophets and teachers... (Acts 13: 1a)

The Miraculous and the Teacher

Signs and wonders should follow their ministry as well as the other offices. Those who are called to this office should expect God to move in their ministries. God always confirms

POWER FOR KINGDOM SERVICE

His word.

The teacher's primary ministry is to expound upon the Word. The Word is most effective when it is taught and demonstrated (signs and wonders following).

The same came to Jesus by night, and said unto him, Rabbi, we know that thou art a teacher come from God: for no man can do these miracles that thou doest, except God be with him. (John 3:2)

Teachers must be careful not to

POWER FOR KINGDOM SERVICE

become so dogmatic that they do not allow the Spirit of God to flow freely. They must guard themselves against skepticism as God moves. They may begin to teach against something that is of God.

In addition, if a teacher is not the senior elder, pastor, or bishop, they have to be careful of the doctrine that they present to others.

POWER FOR KINGDOM SERVICE

Notes:

_____

_____

_____

_____

_____

_____

_____

_____

_____

POWER FOR KINGDOM SERVICE

POWER FOR KINGDOM SERVICE

-Chapter 6-

The Gifts of the Spirit

POWER FOR KINGDOM SERVICE

POWER FOR KINGDOM SERVICE

In this chapter, we will give brief explanations of the gifts of the Spirit listed in I Corinthians 12. For a full explanation of the gifts, they can be discovered in my book, "The Spiritual Gifts: A Biblical Explanation of the Gifts of the Spirit.

The gifts are commonly groups in three divisions: Gifts of Revelation, Gifts of Inspiration, and Gifts of Power.

Gifts of Revelation

Word of Knowledge. It is commonplace today for a believer to

POWER FOR KINGDOM SERVICE

walk up to a brother or sister and say, "I have a word for you." Oftentimes, the individual saying it has no clue what that means. As soon as we hear this expression, we think that a word of prophecy is to follow.

How many of us have been disappointed when it was something we already knew, or they only told us something that we should do? This was because they did not realize they had no word of prophecy, but only a word of knowledge or a word of wisdom.

POWER FOR KINGDOM SERVICE

The word of knowledge is a gift where the Spirit of God reveals facts about individuals and situations from the mind of God.

Word of Wisdom. The word of wisdom is very similar to the word of knowledge, but its function is broader.

The word of wisdom gives us insight into the plan of God and shows us how to apply the word of knowledge. It does what it says; it brings God's wisdom into an individual's life or situation.

POWER FOR KINGDOM SERVICE

Discerning of Spirits. This gift has to be one of the most misunderstood gifts of those listed in I Corinthians 12. To understand the true essence of this gift, we must first understand what it means to discern.

Discern means to differentiate, distinguish, observe, notice, perceive, and note. This shows us that this gift helps the believer to recognize the difference between spirits. It allows believers to know what spirit is behind any given activity.

POWER FOR KINGDOM SERVICE

Gifts of Inspiration

Prophecy. "Thus saith the Lord." This is an expression that some believers cannot wait to hear and an expression that some despise.

In spite of these feelings, God has placed this gift in the body of Christ. It is not only reserved for those who are prophets, but for any believer whom the Spirit will use.

It is a widely publicized gift, but many are still confused about its use, function, and purpose. Whether

POWER FOR KINGDOM SERVICE

through a prophet or layman, prophecy always comes with a purpose. In the most basic terms, prophecy comes with edification, exhortation, and comfort (console).

Divers Kinds of Tongues. Jesus told the disciples that signs would follow anyone who believed. One of the signs was that they would speak with new tongues (Mark 16:17). The fulfillment of this prophecy happened on the day of Pentecost.

And when the day of Pentecost

POWER FOR KINGDOM SERVICE

was fully come, they were all with one accord in one place. And suddenly there came a sound from heaven as of a rushing mighty wind, and it filled all the house where they were sitting. And there appeared unto them cloven tongues like as of fire, and it sat upon each of them. And they were all filled with the Holy Ghost, and began to speak with other tongues, as the Spirit gave them utterance. (Acts 2:1-4)

POWER FOR KINGDOM SERVICE

Since the day of Pentecost, millions have experienced this promised blessing, yet confusion remains as to its purpose and function. There are many facets to this gift. Though we may not understand fully the use and function of this gift, we can narrow its manifestation to three things: prayer, praise, and prophecy.

Interpretation of Tongues. The companion to the gift of tongues is the gift of interpretation of tongues. This gift is necessary to bring understanding

POWER FOR KINGDOM SERVICE

to utterances that are given through the gift of tongues. We have aforementioned that the gift of tongues manifests in three ways: prayer, praise, and prophecy.

Therefore, when an utterance in tongues is given, the interpretation will fall in one of these categories. Many have tried to confine the interpretation of tongues to only expressing a prophetic word.

However, the interpretation of tongues is needed to bring

POWER FOR KINGDOM SERVICE

understanding to expressions of prayer and praise given in tongues. In this way, the whole church is edified, strengthened, and encouraged.

Gifts of Power

Faith. Every believer has been given a measure of faith (Romans 12:3). Yet, certain individuals have the gift of faith and are able to believe God for the impossible. The gift of faith may not be as "spiritual" in its manifestation as the other gifts, yet it produces results.

POWER FOR KINGDOM SERVICE

Individuals possessing this gift will be able to believe God in an unusual way and have the ability to inspire faith in others. Believers with this gift are often times viewed as radical and not in touch with reality. Granted, we have all met people who operate in false faith. Yet, those with the gift of faith will not only believe God for the impossible but will also see the results of this kind of faith.

Gifts of Healings. Along with the gifts of revelation and knowledge, God

POWER FOR KINGDOM SERVICE

has also left gifts of healing to the Church. God also provides relief and freedom from physical ailments through the gifts of healing. It is interesting to note here that the scriptures read "gifts" of healing and not "gift." It is plural.

It is our belief then that there are different manifestations of the gifts of healing. This means that individuals with the gifts of healing may have the ability to heal certain ailments consistently.

POWER FOR KINGDOM SERVICE

Miracles. A miracle is a supernatural act or event. As with the other gifts, miracles are available to believers. Miracles are not the same as healing, as some think.

Miracles are "acts" or events that are strange and abnormal. Though healings may be strange and unusual, they occur through the gifts of healing.

Examples of miracles range from making an axe head float to men walking on water. Paul the apostle had miracles in his ministry.

POWER FOR KINGDOM SERVICE

POWER FOR KINGDOM SERVICE

Bibliography

Lockman Foundation. Comparative Study Bible. Zondervan Publishing House. Grand Rapids, MI, c1984

Tucker, Ron & Hufton, Rick. God's Plan For Christian Service. Grace Church. St. Louis, MO, c1987

The Bible Library. The Bible Library CD Rom Disc. Ellis Enterprises

POWER FOR KINGDOM SERVICE

Incorporated, (c) 1988 – 2000. 4205 McAuley Blvd., Suite 385, Oklahoma City, OK 73120. All Rights Reserved.

Evans, Roderick L. The Spiritual Gifts: A Biblical Explanation of the Gifts of the Spirit. Abundant Truth Publishing. Camden, NC 27921, c2014

POWER FOR KINGDOM SERVICE

The Nine Gifts of the Spirit (I Corinthians 12:4-11)

4. Now there are diversities of gifts, but the same Spirit.

5. And there are differences of administrations, but the same Lord.

6. And there are diversities of operations,

but it is the same God which worketh all in all.

7. But the manifestation of the Spirit is given to every man to profit withal.

8. For to one is given by the Spirit

POWER FOR KINGDOM SERVICE

the word of wisdom; to another the word of knowledge by the same Spirit;

9. To another faith by the same Spirit; to another the gifts of healing by the same Spirit;

10. To another the working of miracles; to another prophecy; to another discerning of spirits; to another divers kinds of tongues; to another the interpretation of tongues:

11. But all these worketh that one and the selfsame Spirit, dividing to every man severally as he will.

POWER FOR KINGDOM SERVICE

The Ministry Gifts and Purpose (Ephesians 4:11-15)

11. And he gave some, apostles; and some, prophets; and some, evangelists; and some, pastors and teachers;

12. For the perfecting of the saints, for the work of the ministry, for the edifying of the body of Christ:

13. Till we all come in the unity of the faith, and of the knowledge of the Son of God, unto a perfect man, unto the

POWER FOR KINGDOM SERVICE

measure of the stature of the fullness of Christ:

14. That we henceforth be no more children, tossed to and fro, and carried about with every wind of doctrine, by the sleight of men, and cunning craftiness, whereby they lie in wait to deceive;

15. But speaking the truth in love, may grow up into him in all things, which is the head, even Christ:

15. But speaking the truth in love,

POWER FOR KINGDOM SERVICE

may grow up into him in all things, which is the head, even Christ:

Other Ministries/Gifts of the Spirit (Romans 12:4-8)

4. For as we have many members in one body, and all members have not the same office:

5. So we, being many, are one body in Christ, and every one members one of another.

6. Having then gifts differing according to the grace that is given to

POWER FOR KINGDOM SERVICE

us, whether prophecy, let us prophesy according to the proportion of faith;

7. Or ministry, let us wait on our ministering: or he that teacheth, on teaching;

8. Or he that exhorteth, on exhortation: he that giveth, let him do it with simplicity; he that ruleth, with diligence; he that sheweth mercy, with cheerfulness.

www.ingramcontent.com/pod-product-compliance
Lightning Source LLC
Chambersburg PA
CBHW050343010526
44119CB00049B/675